DATE DUE

#47-0108 Peel Off Pressure Sensitive

INTERNET
PIRACY

INTERNET PIRACY

BY LEE HUNNEWELL

Content Consultant
Mia Garlick, General Counsel
Creative Commons

ABDO
Publishing Company

CREDITS

Published by ABDO Publishing Company, 8000 West 78th Street, Edina, Minnesota 55439. Copyright © 2008 by Abdo Consulting Group, Inc. International copyrights reserved in all countries. No part of this book may be reproduced in any form without written permission from the publisher. The Essential Library™ is a trademark and logo of ABDO Publishing Company.

Printed in the United States.

Editor: Jill Sherman
Cover Design: Becky Daum
Interior Design: Lindaanne Donohoe

Library of Congress Cataloging-in-Publication Data
Hunnewell, Lee.
 Internet piracy / Lee Hunnewell.
    p. cm. — (Essential viewpoints)
 Includes bibliographical references and index.
 ISBN-13: 978-1-59928-862-8
1. Copyright infringement—United States. 2. Piracy (Copyright)—United States.
I. Title.

 KF3080.H86 2008
 346.7304'82—dc22

                                                    2007013882

TABLE OF CONTENTS

Patricia Santangelo has been accused of Internet piracy.

RIAA Lawsuits

The Internet is an evolving source of information and entertainment for people spanning the globe. It has revolutionized the way people communicate and do business. Information can be shared faster and is easier to find than ever before.

Internet users can share their digital files with friends or even strangers with just the click of a button. Text, images, audio, and video files all have the potential to circulate among users like wildfire. What's more, Internet technology is constantly being improved. It is becoming easier for people to find the information they are looking for and download it to their hard drives.

The Heart of the Controversy

Much of the information on the Internet is copyrighted. This means that it is illegal to share this information without the permission of the copyright owner. Internet users often violate copyright law when they upload or download copyrighted works found online. Copyright owners have the right to say how and when other people may use their creative work. People pay copyright fees to use books, music, movies, televisions shows, software, and many other types of intellectual property. Many copyright owners feel the need to restrict use of their works online because their works are being shared without their permission.

Recording Industry Association of America

The Recording Industry of America (RIAA) is an organization that represents the U.S. recording industry. Its mission is to promote business and legal actions in support of creativity and financial success for its members.

With such a wealth of information readily accessible online, many Internet users are unsure about what they can and cannot do with the material they find. They worry that the rules suggested by the copyright owners will restrict legal uses of the material. They also worry that restrictions will hinder the development of new online technologies.

THE RIAA's LAWSUITS

In September 2003, Brianna Lahara and Durwood Pickle made newspaper headlines. Both were among 261 people sued by the Recording Industry Association of America (RIAA) for making songs available for free on the Internet. Each defendant faced fines of up to $150,000 per downloaded song.

The RIAA represents recording labels and artists. It released a statement at the time of these lawsuits: "when your product is being regularly stolen, there comes a time when you have to take appropriate action."[1] The issue is known as "Internet piracy." The RIAA defines "piracy" as "the illegal duplication and distribution of sound recordings."[2] Most recordings are protected by copyright. Copyright is a set of laws that protect intellectual property, which are creative works, such as songs or movies.

Mitch Bainwol (RIAA), Jack Valenti (MPAA), LL Cool J (actor and recording artist), and Mike Negra (Mike Video, Inc.) at the Senate hearing on illegal file sharing

The RIAA says that making and giving away copies of copyrighted songs is pirating, or stealing. Internet piracy is using the Internet to make and share these illegal copies.

The RIAA's Point of View

The RIAA and organizations like it refuse to back down. The RIAA wants to remind people that "stealing is still illegal, unethical, and all too frequent in today's digital age."[3] According to their reports, the fact that people are staying at home and downloading music for free means that the music and other entertainment industries are losing billions of dollars every year. The president of the Motion Picture Association of America (MPAA), which represents movie interests, said that fighting Internet piracy was like fighting a

Background on the Lawsuits Against Individuals

On June 25, 2003, an RIAA press release warned Internet users that it was gathering evidence to use as the basis of its lawsuits against individuals. "We'd much rather spend time making music than dealing with legal issues in courtrooms," it said. "But we cannot stand by while piracy takes a devastating toll on artists, musicians, songwriters, retailers, and everyone in the music industry."[4]

The press release specified that it would be targeting uploaders—people who were making music available to other Internet users through various Web sites. While the RIAA is against any form of Internet piracy, the statement revealed that the lawsuits were focused on fighting the distribution, or sharing, of pirated content.

In order to gather the evidence, the RIAA said it planned on using computer software to scan the public directories of music-downloading sites. That means that the RIAA was using the software to find out what songs were available, as well as to identify the Internet service provider (ISP) of the people uploading the songs to the site.

"terrorist war." This emphasizes how high the stakes have become for the entertainment industries. Under the circumstances, the RIAA is convinced that it has a good reason for suing individuals: the situation simply demands it.

Furthermore, the RIAA claims that suing individuals is a last-resort tactic. In the press release announcing the lawsuits, the RIAA pointed out that over the previous few years it had made efforts to inform the public that downloading copyrighted music online is illegal, and that it had made huge amounts of music available online at a low cost. Despite these efforts, the problem continued to worsen. Though the RIAA acknowledged that suing individuals was heavy-handed, it hoped that doing so would serve as an example to people who continued to pirate music:

> We hope that today's actions will convince doubters that we are serious about protecting our rights.[5]

Before 2003 … After 2004

Before it started suing Internet users in 2003, the RIAA was already using the courts to fight Internet piracy. However, pre-2003 lawsuits focused on companies rather than individuals. Among other companies, the RIAA sued Napster, Aimster, and Verizon. Meanwhile, the MPAA has followed the RIAA's lead. The MPAA has been suing individual Internet users since 2004.

That is precisely their point. The entertainment industries want people to know that they have a right to protect their property from theft. For the RIAA, the point is not whether the person being sued is 12 years old with no money, or even that the person may not have known that what they were doing was illegal. According to the RIAA, the point is that a person who takes music for free has stolen it. When the RIAA responded to criticism of the Brianna Lahara case, it made no excuses:

> We know that there are a lot of young people who are using these services and we totally expected that we would end up targeting them. … As we have said from the beginning … there is no free pass to engage in music piracy just because you haven't come of age.[6]

CRITICISM OF LAWSUITS

At the time of the lawsuits, Brianna Lahara was 12 years old and living with her mother in a Bronx housing development. Durwood Pickle, the grandfather of teenagers, was living in Texas. Many felt that suing 12-year-old girls and grandfathers for millions of dollars was not an appropriate action. So, while people may agree that Internet users should not download and share copyrighted songs online, a fiery debate exists as to how to handle this problem.

Since 2003, the RIAA has filed nearly 20,000 suits against individuals for copyright infringement. The cases against Brianna Lahara and Durwood Pickle are examples of why people disagree with the anti-piracy tactics of the recording industry. In fact, Brianna Lahara never knew she was doing anything wrong. Her mother, Sylvia Torres, paid a $29.99 fee to use a music-downloading site. In an interview with CBS News, Ms. Torres said, "If you're paying for it, you're not stealing it, so what is this all about?"[7]

Durwood Pickle felt he was not responsible because his grandchildren and their friends had used his computer to download songs without his permission. "I'm not a computer-type person," he said. "They come in and get on the computer. How do I get out of this?"[8]

Critics of the RIAA argue that the lawsuits are targeting innocent people who don't have a chance

Electronic Frontier Foundation (EFF)

EFF is an organization that defends free speech, privacy, creativity, and consumer rights. Consumer rights are the rights of people who consume, or buy, products. EFF wants to make sure that laws are always friendly for the consumer, rather than for big companies.

against powerful music industries. As of 2006, about 4,500 individuals, including Brianna Lahara, settled their cases out of court. The Electronic Frontier Foundation (EFF) helps protect the people's right to use digital technology. It says that people are forced into paying fines to avoid the huge expense of fighting their cases in court. Individuals are humiliated because paying the fines makes it appear that they are admitting guilt. In addition, they never get a chance to argue their side in court.

"Clean Slate" Program

Before launching a second wave of lawsuits, the RIAA offered a "clean slate" to individuals who admitted to illegal downloading and destroyed those illegal copies. By complying with this agreement and refraining from illegal downloading, individuals would be free from lawsuits.

The EFF argues that lawsuits are not working. Rather than scaring people into changing their behavior, the RIAA is creating enemies out of Internet users. Thousands of people have contributed money to help Brianna Lahara and other individuals pay their settlement fees. There is also no conclusive evidence that the number of illegally downloaded songs is dropping. Instead, illegal sites continue to pop up every day on the Web. Big Champagne is a company that monitors Internet trends. It questions whether the suits are just driving Internet pirates further underground, where they will be even more difficult to find. In other words, is it even possible to control the ways Internet users will push technology in today's world?

An Ongoing Debate

Today, the debate continues to rage between industry representatives and critics of their anti-piracy tactics. However, the lawsuit issue is just one of many sticking points that have come up as people tackle Internet piracy. Theft and punishment are not the only issues at stake. Ultimately, the industries' tactics are in response to large-scale theft of their products. This response has raised troubling questions about justice, freedom of expression, greed, education, and the legal system. The court decisions being made today will regulate the ways in which users will be allowed to use the Internet for years to come.

Those who defend online file sharing do so in order to keep a system that millions of Internet users have come to rely on. They object to the recording industry's tactics, particularly the lawsuits against Internet users who cannot properly defend themselves against the charges. It seems that in a desperate effort to defend different positions, each side has turned against the other, making compromise more difficult.

The issues surrounding online file sharing bring up some complex questions. Is it realistic for the RIAA to demand payment for each copy of a song made in the age of the Internet? On the other hand, are Internet users justified in taking and sharing music for free just because the Internet makes it possible for them to do so? Many voices on both sides of the issue are answering "yes" to both of these questions. In fact, the answer is much more complicated.

Many computer users copy their own CDs to their hard drives and then make their hard drives available to millions of users.

Congress passed the U.S. Copyright Act in 1790.

UNDERSTANDING
COPYRIGHT LAW

opyright is a set of rights regulating
the use of the material that has been
copyrighted. Copyright can be generally understood
as the right to copy. In the United States, copyright
involves the right to reproduce, make derivatives,

publicly display, publicly perform, and publicly digitally perform. Copyright owners control the rights to their works. If someone else wants to use a copyrighted work in any of these ways, the law says that they must first receive permission from the copyright owner.

Copyright protection lasts for a given period of time. Once that time runs out, the work becomes part of the public domain. Works in the public domain are available to anyone who wants to use them. Permission is not required. The original story of *Cinderella* is in the public domain. Walt Disney's character Mickey Mouse is not.

Copyright law is a set of laws that controls anything having to do with copyright. According to the U.S. Constitution, Congress has the power:

> to promote the Progress of Science and useful Arts, by securing for limited Times to Authors and Inventors the exclusive Right to their respective Writings and Discoveries.[1]

This refers to the protection of intellectual property. Intellectual

Parodies

Parodies are generally considered fair use of a copyrighted work. A parody is a work that makes fun of something. Political figures and celebrities are often targets of parody. Parodies can also be made of things such as movies and songs, in which key parts of the movie or song have been changed. A good parody is one that makes changes, but also keeps enough of the original so that it is clear what is being parodied.

property means that a person is the owner of his or her creative work (written, recorded, or invented). It gives people such as authors and inventors the right to say how their work can be used. Congress created laws that gave authors and scientists control over their intellectual property. This was to ensure that these innovators would have more incentive to develop new works and share them with the public.

U.S. COPYRIGHT LAW

On May 31, 1790, Congress approved the first U.S. Copyright Act to encourage learning and intellectual advancement. It gave mapmakers, chart makers, and authors the exclusive right to publish their works. A person who has an "exclusive" right over something is the only person who has that right. The Copyright Act made it illegal for anyone other than the copyright owner to take a published work and republish it elsewhere. No one else had the right to "copy" it without permission or payment. Congress set the copyright term, or the amount of time a work was protected, at 14 years. If the copyright owner was still alive at the end of that time, he or she could ask for another 14 years of protection. Copyright protection lasted at most

This symbol marks copyrighted works.

28 years before a work passed into the public domain.
After that, the work was public property. It belonged
to everyone.

Starting in 1831 and continuing into recent times,
Congress has made several changes to the Copyright
Act. It has set longer term limits and increased the types
of works that can be protected. It has given copyright

owners more rights over their intellectual property. In 1998, Congress passed the Sonny Bono Copyright Term Extension Act. It extended copyright protection to last the life of the author, plus 70 years. This new term limit is important. It means that people can make money from their creative works for much longer than before. Because of this law, the Walt Disney Company still holds copyright on the image of Mickey Mouse, even though Walt Disney died in 1966.

Today, many different types of work can be copyrighted: music, software, graphic designs, plays, newspaper articles,

WIPO Internet Treaties

The World International Property Organization (WIPO) was established in 1967 to create balanced and understandable international intellectual property laws. These laws would protect copyrighted works in every country. The WIPO headquarters is located in Geneva, Switzerland.

The WIPO Copyright Treaty (WCT) and the WIPO Performances and Phonograms Treaty (WPPT) were put forth in 1996. These treaties were written in order to update international copyright laws with consideration to the Internet. Of the 184 countries that are part of WIPO, 62 ratified the WCT and 60 have ratified the WPPT as of 2007.

The WIPO Internet Treaties hope to expand business online by establishing firm international copyright rules. Participating countries will need to upgrade their existing copyright laws in order to protect against the breaking of copy protection technologies and to recognize the copyright owner's rights to control how their work is distributed.

poetry, photo images, building designs, and much more, including unpublished works. Unpublished works are protected even if they have never been published or registered with a government office. They are still considered intellectual property.

COPYRIGHT'S RESTRICTIONS

Early copyright laws restricted the copying of a published work. Now, copyright laws do much more. Today, permission is required to perform a copyrighted play or to play a CD at a public place. In both examples, no one is making a copy of the original work. They are performing and sharing the work. These uses now fall under copyright protection. Even more important to know is that derivative works, which are works based on another work, are also protected. When movie producers make a movie based on a book, they must obtain permission from the copyright owner of the book. If, after that, someone wants to make an action figure based on one of the characters in the movie, that person also has to get permission and may have to pay a

Copyright Act of 1790

Congress modeled the Copyright Act of 1790 after England's Statute of Anne, which set the author's term of copyright at 14 years with the possibility of renewal for another 14 years. The statute also gave the copyright owner the exclusive right to print and reprint a work. It did not control any uses of the work beyond that.

fee to the original copyright owner. Copyright used to control only who could copy a work. It now also controls what can be done with the copy as well.

Fair Use

Permission is not necessary for every use of a copyrighted work. Section 107 in the 1976 Copyright Act introduced the concept of "fair use." Congress said it was fair use to copy works if they were "for purposes such as criticism, comment, news reporting, teaching, scholarship, or research."[2] For example, material quoted for a school project makes fair use of a copyrighted work. Teachers may make fair use of copyrighted materials for nonprofit, educational purposes. Even knowing this, it might still be difficult to decide what is considered fair use of a work.

There are four factors to consider when making decisions about fair use that are put forth by Section

Copyright Extension

The Sonny Bono Copyright Term Extension Act added 20 years to the copyright term, which is now life plus 70 years. The main reason Congress decided on the extension was to be consistent with what European nations were already doing. The European Union had already set the copyright term at life plus 70 years. Since U.S. copyright protection lasted life plus 50 years at the time, Europeans were using American works without permission 20 years before they could have used their own works. Congress decided that American intellectual property ought to benefit from protection for the same period of time as did European works.

107 of the Copyright Act. First is the purpose of the use. Using copyrighted material to create a brand new theory or idea is fair use. Second is the nature of the work, such as whether it is fiction or nonfiction. Third is the amount and importance of the work. Generally, using only a small percentage of the work is considered fair use. However, copying only the most meaningful parts of a book or a software program may not be a fair use. Fourth is the effect the use has on the market for, or value of, the original work. Today, the movie and music industries are upset because they believe they are losing billions of dollars to file sharing. Determining fair use is a matter of weighing all these factors and deciding which direction the balance tips.

Copyright and Digital Material

Copyright extends to digital works as well. President Clinton signed the No Electronic Theft Act (NET Act) into law on December 16, 1997. The NET Act makes it a crime to reproduce, distribute, or share copies of copyrighted works over the Internet. The law applies even if the person using the works is not making money from it. The NET Act reversed the requirement that a person had to be making money in order to face criminal copyright infringement charges. As a result of

Work-for-hire

A work-for-hire is a work for which the actual author is not the legal author. In other words, the actual author is not the copyright owner of the work. For example, if a company asks an employee to write a computer program or a paper, the company usually owns the copyright. The actual author may or may not receive personal credit for the work. The copyright term for works-for-hire is set at 95 years after its publication or 120 after its creation. Copyright ends on whichever of these two dates comes first.

this law, more individuals may be punished.

Despite these laws, files are often copied and shared with exponentially more individuals digitally than they are physically. Copyright laws may have to be reformed to take online usage of copyrighted works into greater consideration.

During his presidency, Bill Clinton signed several laws that helped
extend copyright protection to the Internet.

Protestors demonstrate outside the U.S. Supreme Court.

OVERVIEW OF
THE CONTROVERSY

The debate over online file sharing and Internet piracy is a heated one. Individuals representing the entertainment industries argue that piracy is eating into their profits and that the real losers will be consumers. However, organizations that support file sharing criticize the industries' reports. They feel that file sharing encourages creativity more than it hurts the industries.

Opposed: File Sharing Results in Profit Losses

People in the music, film, software, and video game industries are paying close attention to how online file sharing is affecting them. They are writing annual reports estimating how much money they are losing to illegal downloading. They are also researching the age of the average Internet pirate, and how often they pirate. The industries take the findings very seriously and design anti-piracy strategies based on these reports. Dan Glickman, president of the Motion Picture Association of America (MPAA), said that "Piracy is the greatest obstacle the film industry currently faces."[1]

This statement is the MPAA's reaction to estimates that the

Campus Piracy

On September 26, 2006, leaders from the entertainment industries and universities spoke to a U.S. House of Representatives subcommittee about Internet piracy on campuses. The subcommittee chairman said, "The university environment creates a perfect storm for piracy. College students, who are computer and Internet savvy, use state-of-the-art computers and the fastest computer networks in America to find the music, movies, and other entertainment products that they love."[2] At the meeting, the leaders discussed ways to solve the problem through increased education, and the House of Representatives agreed to support this effort.

American movie industry lost $2.3 billion to Internet piracy in 2005. The Recording Industry Association of America (RIAA), the Entertainment Software Association (ESA), and the Business Software Alliance (BSA) represent copyright owners in their specific industries. They are all reporting annual losses in the billions. An RIAA representative estimated that recording artists and labels lose millions of dollars a day to all forms of piracy, including Internet piracy. The BSA says that for every two dollars spent on computer software in 2005, one dollar's worth was pirated.

OPPOSED: INTERNET USERS ARE NOT CONCERNED WITH COPYRIGHTS

There are also many signs that there has been a major change in attitude concerning copyrighted materials. A reported 48 million Americans admit to regularly downloading protected works on the Internet. However, many do not think they are doing anything wrong. In 2002, the *New York Times* reported that a growing number of young people saw the Internet as a huge, free "personal video library."[3] Today, college students are responsible for downloading 44 percent of illegally pirated movies every year. According to the RIAA, half of the college students in a poll did not know if their schools had rules about downloading copyrighted works.

In addition, many people do not feel very sorry for copyright owners and the big industries that back them. Actors and musicians are still leading more glamorous lives than the average person. Studios are still spending hundreds of millions of dollars making movies. With these images in mind, the average Internet user may not see how the billions lost through piracy are having a negative effect.

Opposed: Small Artists Lose Out

Industry representatives have gone out of their way to convince the public that the damage from Internet piracy is widespread. Piracy affects not only the people in the industries but also small artists, local business people, and consumers. For example, the RIAA explains that most musical recordings cost more to make than they earn. As a result, record companies rely on the success of the top 15 percent of their artists in order to make a profit.

The RIAA claims that recording labels use the profits of the 15 percent of CDs that make money to cover the losses of the other 85 percent. This makes record companies less willing to work with smaller artists.

Opposed: Industries Provide Jobs

The MPAA estimates that it provides 750,000 people with jobs. This includes the actors, make-up artists, writers, drivers, extras, and delivery people. These crews also contribute to community businesses in the cities in which they work. The MPAA's main message is that hundreds of thousands of people are at risk of losing their jobs if Internet piracy continues.

Estimated Losses

The MPAA estimates that they suffer $6.1 billion in annual losses from piracy. The U.S. 2005 Piracy Fact Sheet, published by the MPAA, reports that out of the $6.1 billion, $4.8 billion (80 percent) resulted from piracy in other countries, and $1.3 billion (20 percent) resulted from losses in the United States. About $2.3 billion worth of video was believed to be pirated in 2005.

The BSA reports similar effects on software dealers worldwide. They are unable to compete with the prices of pirated materials (free) and are not making profits. According to the ESA, decreasing piracy by a tenth would create 2.4 million new jobs all over the world.

Opposed: File Sharing Hurts Consumers

The industries insist that the biggest victims of Internet piracy will be consumers. These are people who enjoy their products, but who might also be downloading them for free. For one, the quality of pirated recordings are often inferior. Songs and movies frequently cut off too soon. Video games and software may not work properly. The RIAA reminds consumers that pirated recordings cannot be returned if they do not work properly. Downloading from unknown users also puts computers at risk for getting viruses.

In addition, prices for legal CDs will increase. Record companies say they will increase prices to make up for the money they are losing through piracy. Another problem that often results from illegal downloading is that it slows down computer networks, like the ones on college campuses.

In Favor: Reports of Sales Increase

Broadcast Music, Inc. (BMI) represents artists such as Mariah Carey, Kanye West, and Pink. It reported a seven percent increase in sales between 2005 and 2006. These sales were following an upward trend from previous years. Disney's profits doubled in the same time period. ESA reports show that video game sales increased steadily from 2000 to 2004, before dipping some in 2005. Finally, the software industry acknowledges that it is experiencing stable growth.

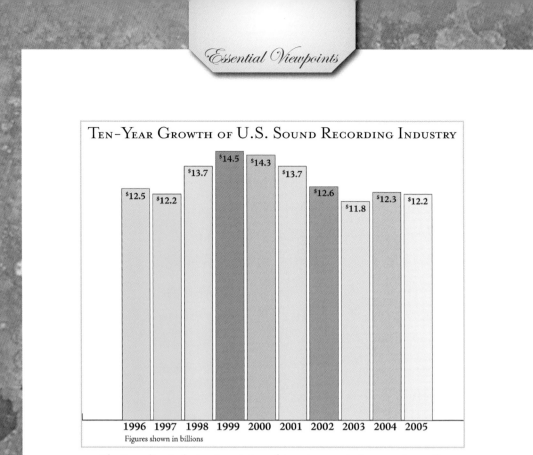

TEN-YEAR GROWTH OF U.S. SOUND RECORDING INDUSTRY

1996	1997	1998	1999	2000	2001	2002	2003	2004	2005
$12.5	$12.2	$13.7	$14.5	$14.3	$13.7	$12.6	$11.8	$12.3	$12.2

Figures shown in billions

The Recording Industry Association of America reports its annual growth.

These numbers suggest that the industries are perfectly healthy, despite illegal downloads.

The music industry is rapidly growing in the digital market. RIAA members are testing different ways to distribute digital music, such as kiosks, downloads, and digital videos. Sales from these distributions have risen by 87 percent. The music industry also found that more people are choosing to buy single song titles. Sales in this market have increased by 71 percent. At the same time, full album sales have increased by 112 percent in

2006. That means they sold more
than twice as many full digital albums
in the first half of 2006 than in the
same time period in 2005. The
number of people using subscription
services also rose by 45 percent.

In Favor: Innovators Lose Opportunities

Lawsuits issued by industries have
tried to shut down companies like
Kazaa, whose technologies allow for
illegal file sharing. Although Kazaa
still operates, it no longer allows
copyrighted content to be shared.
Smaller start-up companies, however,
would not survive lawsuits.

Lawrence Lessig, a Stanford
University professor, claimed, "The record labels have
launched lawsuits against every company that has a
model for distributing [music and entertainment]
content they can't control." In his opinion, lawsuits
such as those intimidate innovators who might have
developed new and useful technologies. Instead,
technological development is being controlled by the

Worldwide Piracy

In 2005, the Business Software Alliance (BSA) reported that the country with the highest software piracy rate, including Internet piracy, was Vietnam. Next came Zimbabwe, Indonesia, and China. The United States came in at the bottom of the list with the lowest software piracy rate. Members of the entertainment industry also estimate huge loses overseas to piracy. As a result, they work with officials in other countries to develop better anti-piracy strategies.

industries. Lessig predicts, "before we know it, the possibility for innovation will have disappeared."[7]

In Favor: Industries Should Adapt

The affected industries are trying to put an end to piracy with lawsuits and copy protection technology. These tactics are often criticized. Many believe that consumers will continue to search for ways to get the material they want. Consumers are using digital material more and more. For example, music fans will often listen to music on their computers, their cars' CD players, and portable media

Artists' Opinions

Opposed

Shakira: "Making an album is a team effort, so when somebody pirates a record that not only affects the artist, but also the people who worked on it like co-producers, co-writers and musicians."

Sean (P. Diddy) Combs: "As an artist who has dedicated his life to music and the music business, I have seen what illegal music copying has done and continues to do to new and established musicians. ... Every single day we're out here pouring our hearts and souls into making music for everyone to enjoy. What if you didn't get paid for your job?"[4]

In favor

Lily Allen: "It's such a powerful thing, to just send your stuff out there into the ether and to get such a massive response."[5]

Moby: "How can a 14-year-old who has an allowance of $5 a week feel bad about downloading music produced by multimillion-aire musicians and greedy record companies?"[6]

players. When consumers purchase music, they want it to be easily used on all of these different formats. Copy protection technology sometimes prevents this.

Critics argue that the industries need to offer consumers more affordable ways to download their material legally. The Internet will continue to be a tool that many consumers turn to. They argue that the industries need to work with developing technologies rather than fight them.

Pirated Software

The BSA warns of more ways in which Internet piracy could affect consumers. Pirated software is not open to technical support or permitted to download the latest upgrades to the original program. So, once the software gets old, it is officially outdated.

IN FAVOR: SMALL ARTISTS GAIN EXPOSURE

RIAA critics believe the exposure that lesser-known artists gain from Internet downloads helps them gain a larger fan base. In the end, this could help lesser known artists become more successful than they might otherwise have been.

Many artists have become successful in this way. Singer Lily Allen posted some of her recordings to her MySpace account prior to the release of the record. In this way, Allen, a relative unknown, was able to gain a larger fan base. Before Allen had released a single record, her music had already developed a following. Artists like Allen have the ability to reach thousands more listeners online than they would through traditional means.

Music listeners can easily search for new artists online. They can sample a new artist's music for free. They can decide for themselves whether they want to purchase the album.

In Favor: Industry Reports Are Misleading

If someone steals a CD, DVD, video game, or software package off the shelf in a store, there is one less item to sell. The industries claim that downloading copyrighted products from the Internet amounts to the same thing: one less sale for them. According to Lawrence Lessig, the industries' profit numbers prove that this is not true.

Even though statistics show that hundreds of millions of their products have been downloaded, their sales numbers have not plunged. Instead, they have dipped, bounced back, and dipped again. This trend could be explained by many other factors. Based on this reasoning, downloading a song off the Internet is not quite the same as stealing a CD outright.

Some consumers buy used CDs as a source for inexpensive music.

Cary Sherman, president of the RIAA, talks to reporters about Internet piracy.

KEY PLAYERS IN
THE CONTROVERSY

There are numerous players on both sides of the online file sharing issue. They have at least one thing in common: they are passionate about the issue. They spend a great deal of time and money making sure their opinions are heard.

Opposed: Recording Industry Association of America

The Recording Industry Association of America (RIAA) represents the U.S. recording industry. Its mission is to promote business and legal actions in support of its members' creativity and financial success. Its membership includes dozens of major labels, such as Atlantic, Sony, Warner Brothers, Motown, numerous smaller labels, and a handful of individual artists. According to the RIAA, its members "create, manufacture and/or distribute approximately 90% of all legitimate sound recordings produced and sold in the United States."[1] That means that nine out of ten songs exist in some way because of the efforts of an RIAA member label or artist.

The president of the RIAA is Cary Sherman. He is a Harvard Law School graduate who has been described in *National Journal* as one of the top copyright attorneys in the country. Sherman also acts as

The MPAA Works All Over The World

Because the piracy problem is worldwide, the MPAA has international branches in Canada, Latin America, Europe (which oversees actions in Africa and the Middle East), and Asia. Through these branches, the MPAA works with local police and lawmakers in affected countries to make arrests, conduct property seizures, and promote strong intellectual property laws.

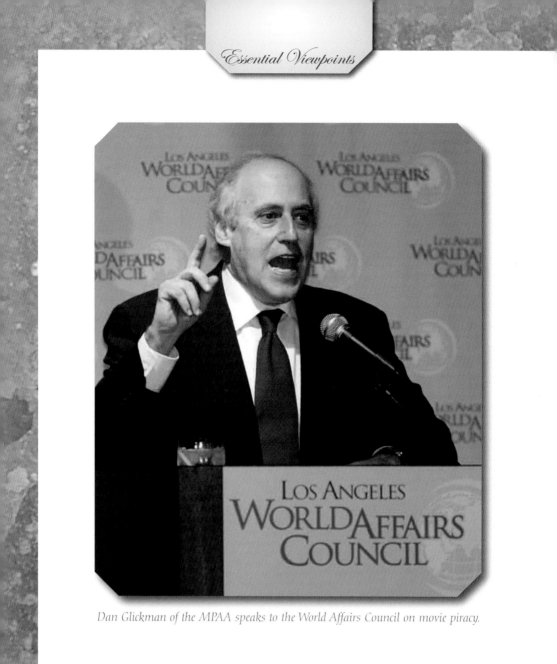

Dan Glickman of the MPAA speaks to the World Affairs Council on movie piracy.

General Counsel for the RIAA. This means that he is the lawyer who represents the organization in all legal processes. Sherman keeps with the RIAA's mission to promote a legal climate that favors its membership. In

2003, Sherman coordinated the push to sue individuals and has unapologetically supported it ever since:

> *The law is clear and the message to those who are distributing substantial quantities of music online should be equally clear—this activity is illegal, you are not anonymous when you do it, and engaging in it can have real consequences.*[2]

The lawsuit and other initiatives he has supported have met with criticism. However, his clear and authoritative manner shows he is determined to protect intellectual property rights.

OPPOSED: MOTION PICTURE ASSOCIATION OF AMERICA

The Motion Picture Association of America's (MPAA) mission is to "serve as the voice and advocate of the American motion picture, home video, and television industries."[3] Like the RIAA, the MPAA supports strong copyright laws and is, among other things, also suing individuals as a way to fight Internet piracy. Members of the MPAA include Sony Pictures Entertainment Inc., Warner Brothers Entertainment Inc., Twentieth Century Fox Film Corporation,

The RIAA Works All over the World

The RIAA has worked in cooperation with the International Federation of the Phonographic Industry (IFPI) since 1999. The IFPI represents the recording industry internationally. Its 1,400 members are spread across 70 countries. Its headquarters is in London, with other offices in Miami, Moscow, Hong Kong, and Brussels. IFPI works with lawmakers and law enforcement in an effort to fight music piracy globally.

Universal City Studios LLP, Paramount Pictures Corporation, and Buena Vista Pictures Distribution, which is The Walt Disney Company.

Dan Glickman took over the presidency of the MPAA in 2004. A former member of Congress, he also served as the Secretary of Agriculture in the Clinton administration. As a former politician, he is in an excellent position to defend the MPAA's viewpoints in front of lawmakers in Congress.

In one statement before a Congressional Committee, Glickman argued that the interests of the MPAA and the government were similar:

> *Protecting the copyright industries and the intellectual property they are based upon goes hand in hand with protecting the U.S. economy and job market.*[4]

Opposed: Business Software Alliance

The Business Software Alliance (BSA) represents the world's software industry in the government and the international marketplace. That means the BSA tries to make the government see the software industry's side of things. The BSA also advertises and sells its products at a good price all over the world. In doing so, the BSA says it is "dedicated to promoting a safe and legal digital world."[5] According to the alliance, minimizing the number of computer viruses is one of many ways in which to create a safe digital world. Pirated software is more likely to contain viruses. This is one reason why the BSA spends its own time and money fighting Internet piracy.

Robert Holleyman, the president of BSA, is a Stanford Business School graduate. He has spent eight years serving the U.S. Senate as a lawyer. Named one of the 50 most influential people in the intellectual property world, Holleyman spends much of his time

EFF Involves the Community in Its Work

EFF's online Action Center gives concerned people an opportunity to support EFF's cause directly. The Action Center lists several digital media issues being debated by Congress, and provides prepared letters of protest to sign and send to appropriate representatives. People can also subscribe to EFF's newsletter and receive "action alerts" that describe new actions of interest in Congress.

making sure that lawmakers in Washington, D.C. pay attention to the issues surrounding intellectual property, including Internet piracy. He runs a series of meetings with high-level members of the government to discuss the BSA's interests. He also frequently appears on television and writes articles for publication around the world. One of Holleyman's main messages is that "it is critical that public policies promote innovation through strong intellectual property protection."[6] In other words, successful software development depends on how strong the laws are that protect the technology.

World Intellectual Property Organization

WIPO is an international organization. Its mission is to promote the protection of intellectual property. WIPO attempts to enhance the enjoyment of life while creating greater wealth for nations. WIPO places itself on the side of both intellectual property owners and the general public that is enjoying the creative works of these owners.

WIPO is headquartered in Geneva, Switzerland, and has a membership of 183 countries. It oversees 24 international intellectual property treaties, including the Rome Convention of 1961, which granted copyright protection to performances, phonograms, and television broadcasts.

The Geneva staff represent more than 90 countries and include people active in law, economics, public policy, information technology (IT), and administration. WIPO's main tasks include developing international intellectual property laws and standards and educating the public about intellectual property issues.

In Favor: Electronic Frontier Foundation

The Electronic Frontier Foundation (EFF) is one of the strongest voices on the other side of the online file sharing issue. It is an organization that defends free speech, privacy, creativity, and consumer rights. Consumer rights are the rights of people who consume, or buy, products. EFF works to make sure that laws are as consumer-friendly as they are corporation-friendly. To do so, it files and defends lawsuits. These include lawsuits against the government and organizations such as the RIAA. EFF also organizes activist groups, advises lawmakers, and develops educational programs for the public.

The Board of Directors, or group of people who manage the EFF, includes professors, technologists, and lawyers, such as Stanford University's Lawrence Lessig. Lessig has defended cases in front of the U.S. Supreme Court. He has written about copyright law and its impact on freedom of expression. In his book,

Creative Commons Going International

Creative Commons is now operating in 35 countries, giving copyright owners in those countries an opportunity to more actively choose the limits on their licenses. Ongoing work is happening to launch Creative Commons in Turkey, Bangladesh, Guatemala, and Tanzania.

Free Culture, Lessig argues that copyright laws should respect both the rights of copyright owners and the rights of people to create. Copyright law is about balancing these rights. He also argues that a certain amount of piracy is necessary for creativity's sake. It is an undeniable part of the entertainment industry's past, he claims.

> *If "piracy" means using the creative property of others without their permission ... then the history of the content industry is a history of piracy. ... The film industry of Hollywood was built by fleeing pirates.* [7]

In Favor: Free Software Foundation

The Free Software Foundation (FSF) supports the use of free computer software. Its mission is to:

> *preserve, protect and promote the freedom to use, study, copy, modify, and redistribute computer software, and to defend the rights of all free software users.* [8]

FSF runs its programs using the monetary contributions of individual members. Current FSF projects include building a free software directory and supporting free software developers. It also supports the GNU project, a free computer operating system.

Richard Stallman is the president and founder of FSF. He is a graduate of Harvard University and was a "staff hacker" at the Massachusetts Institute of Technology (MIT) Artificial Intelligence Lab. Stallman has won awards for his software development, including the Pioneer Award from EFF. He has also been awarded honorary degrees at universities around the world. In defending his position that software should be free, Stallman points out that the copyright system was developed for printed materials. "An ordinary reader," he says, "could copy books only with pen and ink, and few readers were sued for that." He argues that the Internet age and the copyright system are a "bad fit." He says this is the reason "for the increasingly nasty … measures now used to enforce software copyright."[9]

In Favor: Creative Commons

Creative Commons is an organization with a goal "to build a layer of reasonable, flexible copyright in the face of increasingly restrictive default rules."[10] This means that they offer copyright owners an alternative way to register their works. Obtaining a copyright license from Creative Commons means that an owner could set these works free for certain uses. For example, a photographer could choose to make his work available for free as long as his name was credited. With these alternate copyright licenses, Creative Commons is looking to rebuild the balance between copyright owner's rights and the people's right to access information.

Lessig runs Creative Commons and also sits on its Board of Directors. Other directors are experts in intellectual property and computer technology, lawyers, and business owners. Support for their work comes from individual donors and corporate and foundation donors. Donors include Microsoft, Google, the U.S. Department of State, and the Rockerfeller Foundation.

Lawrence Lessig is involved in organizations such as the EFF and Creative Commons.

Mark Russinovich found copy protection issues with Sony music CDs.

COPYRIGHT IN
THE DIGITAL AGE

O n October 28, 1998, President Clinton
signed the Digital Millennium Copyright
Act (DMCA) into law. This represented a major victory
for entertainment industries. The industries are
looking to strengthen copyright law as part of their

anti-piracy work. Among other things, the DMCA makes it illegal to circumvent copy protection or to distribute tools that make circumvention possible. Circumventing something means finding a way around it. The DMCA makes it illegal for people to get around copy protection technologies on DVDs and other digital media. The copy protection technologies are designed to prevent people from making copies of these products. The DMCA also makes it illegal to create, sell, or distribute technologies that make it easier to get around copy protection.

Like the education and law enforcement tactics used by the industries, strong laws such as the DMCA and the legal cases they produce cause huge disagreements between people.

Who Does Copyright Protection Technology Help?

According to the industries, the DMCA protects artists and the consumers of their products. They

Copy Protection

In November of 2005, Sony had to take millions of its CDs off store shelves. The copy protection technologies it had built into its CDs were putting computers at risk for viruses. Facing lawsuits and fines, Sony agreed to fix the technology as well as to make any new technology more friendly to the concept of fair use. For example, it had to make the songs on its CDs available through at least three types of downloading services.

argue that installing copyright protection technology into DVDs, CDs, and computer hard drives would be a huge help in the fight against piracy. It would create an "anti-piracy infrastructure." This means there would be one protection system that everyone had to use. Having one system would make it easier to control how digital material is used. Artists would be more likely to publish their work on legal downloading sites. The Business Software Alliance (BSA) says that a strong DMCA means a "safe and legal online world," and adds that the "abundance of creative content online is proof that the DMCA is working."[1] In other words, the BSA believes that because there are a lot of creative works available online, artists are confident the DMCA will keep people from hacking into their works. The industries say that this "safe and legal online world" means the DMCA is good for artists and Internet users.

The BSA also says that the DMCA has improved the Internet. It has done this "through both the distribution of content and the correct digital rights to protect such material."[2] In other words, because of the DMCA, there are more legal sites selling reliable products. At the same time, programmers now have a reason to create new and better copyright protection technology. This helps, not hurts, scientific research. The BSA reports a U.S. Copyright Office study on the effects of the DMCA. This study "confirms that there is no need or justification for changing the anti-circumvention provisions of the DMCA."[3]

PROBLEMS WITH COPYRIGHT PROTECTION TECHNOLOGY

One problem with the DMCA is that it gives industries control over how consumers use products at home. If a CD is copy protected it may not play on a computer or be transferred to an MP3 player. The owner cannot get around the technology that keeps the CD from working on those machines. The EFF believes this means that consumers suffer as a result.

In addition, the "abundance of creative content online" may be just a list of what the industries are blocking access to. Copy protection limits what the user can do with the product and restricts where it can end up. The industries are making it illegal to get around copy protection technology. Laws such as the DMCA make it easier to control what ends up on the Internet. It allows for punishment of anyone who puts those materials online because that person has clearly cracked codes that protect the work.

Punishing people under the law for breaking copy protection technology may lead to terrible consequences. The DMCA weakens the concept of fair use. This means more and more people have to circumvent technology in order to use the products they have purchased. The EFF warns that as a result of the DMCA, fair users are now being found guilty for "picking the lock." The big picture is that people are less free to use their own products and to create new products.

FINDING A BALANCE

Copyright owners can control certain uses of their works,

SDMI Challenge

On September 6, 2000, the Secure Digital Music Initiative (SDMI) challenged "the digital community" to break new security systems. The goal of the challenge was to test the strength of the new security technologies.

Edward W. Felten took up the challenge, discovered weaknesses in a security device known as the Verance Watermark, and planned on publishing his results in a scientific paper. The RIAA sent Felten a letter warning him that he could face a DMCA lawsuit if he published the paper. He had signed an agreement stating that he would hack only a limited list of music files. They argued that if Felten published the paper, he would be encouraging people to attack music files. According to the RIAA, the scientific paper would amount to a circumvention tool.

Felton published his paper in 2001 and, backed by the EFF, filed a lawsuit against the RIAA, asking a court to declare that publishing his paper was not against the law. Representatives of the RIAA said that they never had any intention of suing Felten, but had sent him the letter out of obligation to their client, Verance Corporation. In November 2002, the courts, questioning the validity of the suit, chose not to hear the case.

but consumers are permitted
to use the works in ways that are
considered fair use. This balance
is important for copyright laws to
work. Opponents to the DMCA
criticize the law for the amount
of control it gives copyright owners.
It limits what is considered fair
use. In their opinion this has
shifted the balance in favor of
copyright owners.

In 2003, Congressman Rick
Boucher introduced the Digital
Media Consumers' Rights Act
(DMCRA) to Congress. This bill
would amend the DMCA to allow
anti-circumvention for legal uses
of the copyright work. People who
circumvent technology in order to violate copyright
laws would still be breaking the law.

The DMCA makes it a crime to distribute tools that
make circumvention possible. This applies even if they
can be used for fair use purposes. DMCRA supporters
say that under the DMCA, new and important
technologies are at risk of being made illegal.

DMCA

DMCA was introduced to Congress in 1997 and sponsored by Representative Howard Cobble from North Carolina. Included in the DMCA text was a guarantee that the law should be reviewed within a two-year period. The review, among other things, would determine the extent to which the DMCA had stopped copyright violations. In general, the reviews were mixed, acknowledging both the law's successes and its failures.

DMCA Exceptions

In October of 2003, the Library of Congress created some exceptions to the DMCA anti-circumvention law. For example, access control measures may be circumvented in order to use computer programs that are protected by damaged or out-of-date technology. It can also be broken to use programs or video games that were built using technologies that no longer work on new computers. Also, computer users may circumvent access control measures in an e-book so that they can put it in a format that people with disabilities can use.

DISTINGUISHING BETWEEN FAIR AND ILLEGAL USES

The entertainment industries are against the DMCRA. They say the DMCRA has nothing to do with fair use. Instead, they think that passing the DMCRA would make a joke out of the DMCA. This is because existing technology cannot tell whether copy protection is being broken for fair use or illegal purposes.

At the Congressional hearing, the MPAA president argued that legalizing some types of circumvention would not benefit fair use. According to him, fair use was "alive and well." He felt that the DMCRA would cause piracy to explode. The industries would lose the right to continue certain circumvention lawsuits. The public would also gain the right to hack their products.

Volunteers destroy pirated CDs and DVDs as part of
the Philippine government's anti-piracy campaign.

China is one of the leading sources for pirated movies and software.

ONLINE TECHNOLOGIES
IN USE

The MPAA reports that nearly 90 percent of pirated movies begin with someone in a movie theater holding a camcorder. Representatives of the software, music, and video game industries say that those who pirate their products begin in similar ways. They get a hard copy, sometimes standing in line to buy it, and then release it to the Internet. They can do this by uploading it themselves or by sending the products to organized release groups. These groups are known as Warez groups. They operate Warez sites, which are like giant supermarkets for pirated works.

FILE SHARING

Warez sites are just the first stop for pirated products. Soon, the pirated materials find their way to peer-to-peer (P2P) networks. Millions of people can access these networks. In the first P2P networks, file sharers connected to a central server. The server hosted a list of files that were available from other computers that were also connected to the server at that time. Users could download files from other computers that were connected to the server.

Most P2P networks today are decentralized. BearShare, eMule, and Morpheus are some popular decentralized P2P networks. Decentralized networks do not have

FTP Sites

Internet users use file transfer protocol (FTP) sites to transfer files from one computer or server to another. In order to get a file from a computer, the user needs to know the computer's name, and have a user name and password. Software pirates use FTP sites because they are capable of storing large amounts of files, and the files transfer fairly easily from one computer to the next.

a central server. Instead there are multiple nodes that connect to one another when a user does a search. Once the user finds what they are looking for, they can download that file.

BitTorrents work in a similar way. BitTorrents are designed to handle larger files, such as software, videos, and video games. Users have to search for the files on their own because there is no central network. The number of users sharing the same file affects the speed that it can be downloaded. However, rather than downloading the entire file from one user, BitTorrents take pieces of the same file from multiple users. With millions of people connected to P2P networks, users have access to as many files as

Effectiveness of Lawsuits

According to BigChampagne, a company that studies online media trends, punishing individuals and threatening them with impossible fines does not work. The company found that "File sharing has never been more popular than it is now. … People have heard all the legal threats … but that's not enough."[1] Even though the industries have filed thousands of lawsuits, statistics say that P2P usage has doubled in that same amount of time.

The RIAA and other industry representatives disagree. They say the lawsuits are working, that people are finally understanding the consequences of pirating. Several months after it began suing individuals, the RIAA released a statement that said that "a variety of experts suggest traffic on the illegal peer-to-peer network sites is down."[2] It also reported that, since announcing the lawsuits, Internet users had contacted the RIAA admitting to pirating and asking if there was anything they could do to avoid being sued.

exist on those millions of desktops.

Other sites, such as YouTube, host pages where users can post video clips. YouTube manages the traffic of people visiting the pages. The difference between P2P networks and YouTube is that people have access only to what has been uploaded to the server. Users can only watch videos at the YouTube site and cannot download them to their hard drives.

FORCING DOWN COPYRIGHT MATERIAL

The industries can, and often do, spend the time and money forcing Web sites to remove copyrighted material from their pages. Many clips that make it to YouTube are later forced down at the request of copyright owners and industry representatives.

On November 17, 2006, Universal Music Group announced that it was suing MySpace, another Web page hosting site. Universal claimed that "MySpace is a willing partner in ... theft."[3]

E-mail Piracy

Internet pirates can use e-mail to distribute copyrighted software. According to the Business Software Alliance (BSA), software pirates either send the products as attachments, or they write the software code into the text of their messages. This way, they can avoid having to make hard copies. Internet pirates use news and chat groups in similar ways to distribute materials, encoding software or other products into the messages they post.

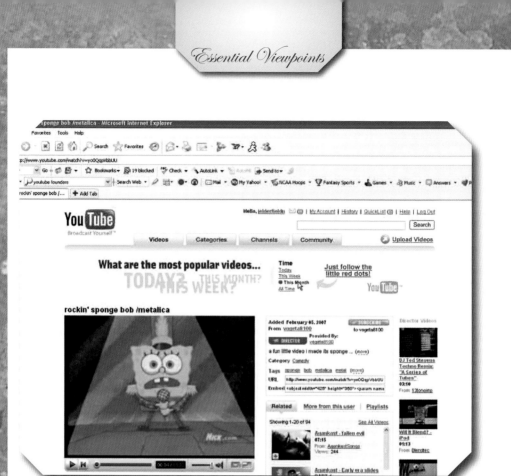

*Nickelodeon owner Viacom Inc. sued the video-hosting site YouTube
for copyright infringement in March 2007.*

Universal is seeking as much as $150,000 for each
posted copyrighted item. Universal will probably be
able to force the copyrighted material off the site, but it
is only a temporary solution. MySpace is just another in
a long line of similar and extremely popular sites. If
MySpace were shut down, there would be many others
ready to take its place, providing the same or very
similar services.

Using Technologies as a Publicity Tool

After airing on December 17, 2005, the *Saturday Night Live* (SNL) skit, "Lazy Sunday," made it onto YouTube. Users viewed this television episode 5 million times. NBC later had YouTube take down the video of the "Lazy Sunday" skit. Shortly after, NBC posted the video on its own site in response to the video's popularity.

A year later, in December 2006, *Saturday Night Live* was losing its popularity. It had lost many of its popular cast members. In response, NBC posted another popular SNL skit directly to YouTube. On this site, it would reach more viewers and help expand their market.

Controlling Content on P2P

It is more difficult for copyright owners to control their work if it is shared on P2P networks. For one thing, P2P vendors do not control the content. They distribute the software but have no control over what is shared. In addition, the content that is available through P2P changes as users connect and disconnect to the network.

Servers

There are several different types of servers. A file server, for example, stores files that many users require access to. These files can then be opened by users on multiple PCs. Other servers manage Web sites. Using a server is like being a customer. The server delivers the file or Web site to whichever PC requests it. Sometimes a username and password are required to access the files.

Darknets

A Darknet is a private network used to communicate and share files. Unlike P2P networks, Darknets usually limit the number of people a user can invite to join their network. Like P2P networks, most of the shared files are protected by copyright. Darknets are networks of people who share copyrighted digital material without making it available to the public at large. People create Darknets because they think that entertainment companies control too much of what the public sees. In other words, they are taking some of this control back.

The industries go about this in two ways: lawsuits against P2P users, and lawsuits against vendors. When an industry sues a P2P user, it is for copyright infringement. When they sue P2P vendors, it is for contributory and vicarious infringement. This means that P2P vendors are responsible for the content being shared on their sites. This is true even if they are not directly sharing any copyrighted material. The industries would like to shut down as many P2P networks as possible in order to stop their copyrights from being violated.

YouTube co-founders Steven Chen, left, and Chad Hurley

Shawn Fanning created Napster when he was a college student.

P2P IN THE COURTS

One of the Recording Industry Association of America's (RIAA) key missions "is to help foster a legal climate that protects the rights of record companies, artists and copyright owners in general."[1] This means that they work to make sure that courts are enforcing copyright laws. The more cases that they win on the basis of a copyright law, the stronger that law will become.

As a result, one of the main ways that the industries fight piracy is to bring companies and individuals to court and try them under existing copyright laws.

NAPSTER: THE BEGINNING OF P2P

In 1998, Shawn Fanning, a college student at Northeastern University, had the idea to build a computer program that would allow him and his friends to share music on their PCs. Two years later, after the program was completed, Fanning became one of the most famous teenagers in the United States. He appeared on the covers of numerous business magazines for his successful peer-to-peer (P2P) file-sharing network, Napster.

Napster put computer desktops that stored music in contact with each other. This made the variety of available music files almost limitless. The Napster server listed song titles and the bandwidth size of the copies available from users who were

RIAA Lawsuit

In 2006, the RIAA brought a lawsuit against a P2P network called LimeWire in *Artista v. Limewire*. In response, LimeWire filed a countersuit with its own claims of antitrust violations against the record companies.

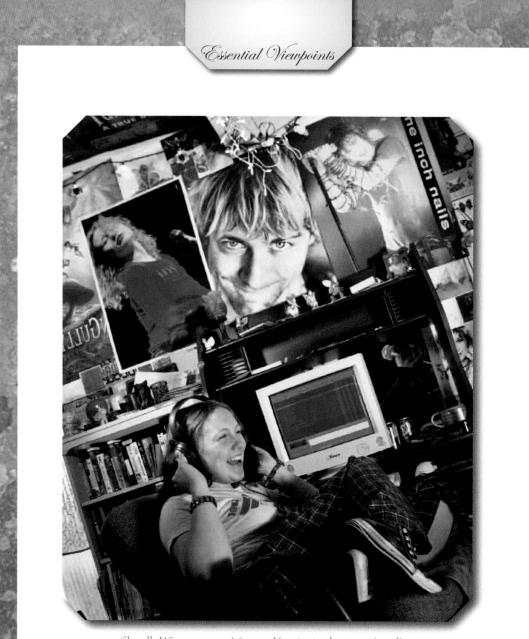

Chevelle Wiseman, age 16, uses Napster to share music online.

connected to the network. Bandwidth is the rate at which files can be transferred from one place to another.

Napster was the first P2P file-sharing network of its kind. In October of 2000, Fanning reported that Napster had 32 million users. He estimated there were 800,000 people using it at any one time. At the same time, site membership was also growing at a rate of 1 million users per week.

A&M Records v. Napster

On December 8, 1999, the RIAA announced it was suing Napster for violating copyright laws. This was the first P2P technology case. This case would set the example for future cases. The RIAA could not accuse Napster of direct infringement. This was because the program did not actually make copies of the songs. Instead, Napster was charged with contributory and vicarious copyright infringement. In other words, Napster was making it possible for others to violate copyright. It was also making no effort to stop its users from doing so.

Barker Case

In January 2007, Tenise Barker moved to dismiss a complaint from the RIAA against her for copyright infringement. Among other things, Barker argued that the RIAA's charge of making copyright material "available" is not actually in violation of copyright law. The RIAA contended that making copyright work available is still copyright infringement even though it is not specifically noted in the Copyright Act. The case is still awaiting a ruling.

Napster's defense argued that their case was very
much like a similar case that was decided in the U.S.
Supreme Court in 1984. Universal Studios sued Sony
for vicarious and contributory copyright infringement
with its video recording machine, the Betamax. The
Betamax was an earlier version of the VCR. Universal
said that the Betamax was being used to make illegal
copies of movies. The Supreme Court ruled against
Universal Studios. They said that Sony probably knew
that their machine could be used for illegal purposes.
However, they could not know of or stop actual cases of
it happening. Second, the Court acknowledged that the
Betamax could be used in many legal ways, so Sony
could not be held responsible when people chose to
use it illegally.

The judges of *A&M v. Napster* found that Napster had
evidence that people were using its program illegally.
The program could not distinguish between legal and
illegal files, but the programmers could. Additionally,
the judges agreed that although Napster had the right
and was capable of stopping the illegal use, it did
nothing to stop it.

The judges did not accept Napster's fair use defense
either. People were copying entire creative works and
exchanging these works with strangers. It was not just

Mitch Bainwol works to strengthen copyright laws as chief executive of the RIAA.

for personal or educative use. The court also found that people using Napster were less likely to buy CDs. This was hurting the music industry's sales. Napster's file sharing service was shut down.

GROKSTER: SECOND GENERATION P2P

After Napster's legal troubles, programmers set out to create new networks. Unlike Napster, these networks would not run off of a central server. Without a main server controlling traffic, the network would be able to grow much larger.

Grokster is one of many second-generation file-sharing programs that became popular after Napster was shut down. Grokster allows users to access the FastTrack P2P network. Kazaa is another program that accesses this network.

Life After Napster

After Napster, the Gnutella P2P network hit the Internet. It connected computers to other computers for file-sharing purposes. One of the main differences between the two networks was that Gnutella had no central server, or system that kept track of song titles available on the network. Instead, Gnutella users searched for titles by asking other users where the files might be found. Though this made for a more difficult search process, taking away the central server meant that the network would be very difficult to shut down. This was not the case for Napster. Once its server shut down, the network fell apart.

The FastTrack P2P network came next. It operated using supernodes, which are temporary servers that search for titles of works. Examples of popular FastTrack clients include Kazaa, Morpheus, and Grokster. As a client of FastTrack, Kazaa identified, connected, and communicated with supernodes in order to fulfill the search requests of ordinary Internet users. This made the search process easier again, without using a central server that could easily be shut down.

P2P technology continues to develop and become more sophisticated, constantly adjusting to the needs of users. There is no evidence to suggest that P2P networks will not exist in some form far into the future.

MGM v. Grokster

In 2003 the RIAA and MPAA
backed a lawsuit against Grokster for
secondary copyright infringement.
Grokster claimed that once they
provided the software, it had nothing
more to do with its use. Grokster
claimed that in this way, its product
was similar to the Betamax. Once
Grokster provided it to the
customer, they had no actual
knowledge of illegal activity.
Grokster also claimed that there were substantial
legitimate, non-infringing uses for its software.

New Law Takes Effect

On April 27, 2005, President Bush signed the Family Entertainment and Copyright Act into law. It included the Artists' Rights and Theft Prevention Act, which made it a crime to use recording equipment to copy movies in theaters.

In April 2003, the court ruled in favor of Grokster,
citing the *Betamax* decision. That decision was appealed
by the RIAA. In August 2004, the Ninth Circuit
Court of Appeals upheld the original ruling in favor
of Grokster.

The case then went to the U.S. Supreme Court. On
June 27, 2005, the Supreme Court ruled against
Grokster for secondary copyright infringement. The
Supreme Court found that Grokster encouraged its
users to break copyright law. Therefore, the *Betamax* case
did not apply.

P2P Networks Persist

Internet users are still choosing peer-to-peer sites to download copyrighted songs, movies, and other products. Despite frequent lawsuits, P2P sites are alive and well.

What's more, they are constantly changing and using new technology. Programmers can modify existing programs to make them faster, more efficient, and more difficult to detect.

Based on the speed with which P2P changes, the courts' decisions may have to be reevaluated and applied to each new development in P2P technology to come. At this rate, a court ruling against file sharing technology may have little lasting effect in the fight against piracy.

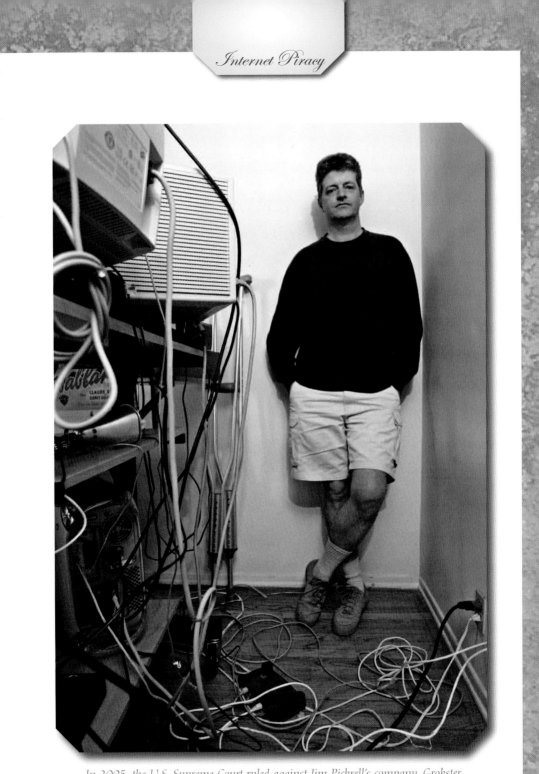

In 2005, the U.S. Supreme Court ruled against Jim Pickrell's company, Grokster.

Software engineers at Musicmatch process CDs to stream online for customers.

AVOIDING PIRACY

Most Internet users have downloaded music, movies, video games, or software at some point. It is important to know how to do so legally. Internet users should be aware that there are many legal sites from which users can buy, rent, and sample products.

Using the Internet responsibly is important. It is up to Internet users to know if what they are doing online is allowed. Users must know the product they are downloading and the Web site they are using in order to be responsible Web users.

RECOGNIZING ILLEGAL COPIES

Although using P2P networks is not illegal, downloading copyrighted material from them is. Unless permission has been obtained, copying, distributing, performing, displaying, or making derivative copies of these products is against the law.

The entertainment industries want consumers to know how to recognize illegal copies of their products. The best way of recognizing a pirated video game, music, or software item on the Internet is to notice if the products are not yet out in theaters or in stores. Knowing the product is key to determining what can be legally downloaded. If the product

The New Napster

Since the 9th Circuit Court of appeals ruled against Napster in February 2001, the company has changed its format and become a legal alternative to P2P. Computers that run on Windows can run Napster, and users can get access to millions of songs. Users can get Napster-made playlists and other downloads that play on compatible MP3 players. They can also get personalized recommendations for what music to add to their collection. Napster advertises itself as "fast, safe, and legal."

must be purchased elsewhere, users will most likely have to pay for the download.

Music Options

There are many legal sites for purchasing downloaded music. Apple's iTunes is perhaps one of the most popular. The site boasts over 3.5 million songs available for download. Users can sample a 30-second clip of the song before purchasing either individual songs or albums. Other sites like eMusic offer subscriptions for a limited number of downloads per month.

Legal Sites for Downloading Music:

Rhapsody
iTunes
MP3 Music Downloads
Full Music Downloads

Another source for online music is to listen to streaming audio files. These files, however, cannot be downloaded to the computer's hard drive, so users are only able to listen to music while they are online.

Movie Options

Many sites are available for consumers to download legal copies of music, movies, and software. Spanning the industries, there are rental sites, viewing or listening sites, and sites that allow users to sample a

Apple Computer's popular iTunes music store boasts over 3.5 million songs.

product before buying it. The MPAA provides a list of them on its Web site. For example, there is CinemaNow, where users can buy movies. Users can download a selection of old movies for free. They can also get a monthly subscription to view "member's only" movies.

Additionally, more and more universities and colleges are partnering with the entertainment industries. They are creating sites that target the needs of the college students, who are the biggest downloaders. For example, Ruckus makes 1.5 million sound recordings and a long list of films available. It also allows members of the community to connect with other members and share these products legally.

SOFTWARE OPTIONS

Various brands of computer software offer free trials. Consumers can test the software before purchasing it on the Internet. Many software companies offer these trial versions of their

Respect Copyrights

In October of 2006, the MPAA and the Boy Scouts of Los Angeles announced their "Respect Copyrights" program. It is a set of activities that teaches troop members that Internet piracy is illegal and that they should respect copyrights. One of the possible activities is playing a video game and finding out who designed it. Another is going to a movie studio and learning about what goes into making a movie. Dan Glickman, head of the MPAA, sees this curriculum as a "real opportunity to educate a new generation about how movies are made, why they are valuable, and hopefully change attitudes about intellectual property theft."[1]

The MPAA hopes that this program will educate youth about copyrights and deter them from copying movies to share with others. However, many feel that the program focuses too much on respecting copyrights and not enough on teaching kids what copyright actually is and how it works. They criticize the MPAA's approach because it focuses too much on what consumers can't do with copyright works as opposed to what they can do.

products on their company's Web sites. CNET offers trial versions of various software applications. It also posts user ratings and reviews.

Legal Sites for Downloading Movies and Games:

IFilm
Movielink
Unlimited Game Downloads
Game Download Now

In addition, open-source software is legal to download from P2P and BitTorrent sites. Open-source software is software in which the programming code is made available to the users. Users are permitted to modify the software as they please. An open-source license also allows for free redistribution of the original software and any of its modified versions. The Linux operating system is an example of open-source software.

CONSUMER RESPONSE

Consumer groups argue that these legal choices are not good choices. According to EFF, the products available from these sites often come with restrictions that limit their use.

For example, music paid for on a legal site may not copy onto all listening devices. Other downloading services only offer the product as long as the user is paying a subscription fee. Once the subscription is canceled, the products that were downloaded are no longer available for users to view, listen to, or use.

Next, the selection of music and films on legal sites is limited. They often do not include lesser-known artists or rare clips. Some popular artists have contracts that restrict them from making their work available on legal sites. Others simply choose not to allow online access to their work. Finally, consumers feel that the prices on legal sites are too high. These prices do not reflect what some people are willing to pay for downloads.

ENTERTAINMENT INDUSTRIES' STANDPOINT

The entertainment industries want consumers to know that there are no alternatives to the legal options currently available. As time goes on, new sites will be available with more options. The RIAA reports that legal music sites quadrupled between 2004 and 2005. Industry statistics show that the number of people using legal sites is growing steadily, reaching an all-time high of 4.2 percent of the "Internet-connected households in December 2005."[2]

The RIAA goes further. It argues that the only way for legal downloading sites to grow and improve is if illegal downloaders continue to be punished for infringing copyright.

Starbucks's new Hear Music media bar allows consumers to burn CDs from the Starbucks music library.

David Weld and Doug Turner of MessageGate Inc. have
designed filtering programs for PCs.

SOLUTIONS THAT
BRIDGE THE GAP

Online file sharing continues to be a topic
of debate. Currently, sharing copyrighted
files on the Internet without proper permission is
illegal. However, Internet users continue to share these
files at alarming rates. Should Internet users be allowed

to share any material they wish? Should the industries be allowed to continue threatening lawsuits against users who violate copyright laws? Are copy protection technologies fair to consumers?

At the moment, the debate over file sharing seems to be a losing battle for all parties involved. The industries continue to report low sales numbers, and file sharers and P2P software developers continue to be targeted for lawsuits. Despite the number of legal sources to download files from on the Internet, many Internet users find these sources unsatisfactory. While most agree that copyright holders deserve to be compensated for their works, the consumers' demand for file sharing networks has yet to decrease.

Although it is clear that Internet piracy is illegal, it is less clear what should be done about it. There are, however, a few possibilities being discussed that could solve the issue for all parties involved. It is possible that a compromise is in sight.

"Would you buy a car which could only drive to five locations on just three roads, required re-purchasing when it broke down, with only three people a day allowed to be passengers and no option for other drivers to use it ... and it cost more than a normal car without all the problems?"[1]

– *Mark Serlin, London UK (Internet user)*

Voluntary Collective Licensing

One solution is to make P2P file sharing legal. Under a system of voluntary collective licensing, copyright owners would have to offer blanket licenses to their work at a reasonable fee. Collective licensing is the way that the music industry earns money for radio-play of their music. The licenses could be offered to Internet Service Providers (ISPs), the P2P software vendors, or the consumers themselves. When the money is collected, it is then distributed among the copyright holders based on the popularity of their music. In exchange for this payment, file sharers would be free to download

---

FAIR USE Act

U.S. Representatives Rick Boucher (Democrat) and John Doolittle (Republican) introduced a new bill on February 27, 2007. The Freedom and Innovation Revitalizing U.S. Entrepreneurship (FAIR USE) Act is meant to allow certain instances of circumvention of digital copy restrictions. The FAIR USE Act would allow exemptions to the restrictions in the DMCA.

Boucher hopes that this bill will restore some of the balance between copyright owners and those who use copyright material. According to Boucher, the DMCA is too strong. He contends that the balance leans toward complete copyright protection, and the the DMCA unfairly limits the public's right to fair use.

The RIAA sees things differently. They believe that by allowing anticircumvention the FAIR USE Act would "allow electronics companies to induce others to break the law for their own profit."[2] With this act in place, they feel that more consumers will be likely to infringe copyright.

anything they like without fear of lawsuits.

The EFF has proposed this compromise, stating,

> the vast majority of file sharers are willing to pay a reasonable fee for the freedom to download whatever they like, using whatever software suits them.[3]

They suggest a fee of $5 per month. If the 60 million P2P software users paid this fee, it would result in $3 billion for the music industry.

However, the music industry doubts the efficiency of this system and the willingness of users to pay. Voluntary collective licensing only works if all copyright owners join. If copyright owners refused to license their work, the government could step in and require licensing. The U.S. government has done this in the past on a few occasions. In the end, the decision lies in the hands of Congress.

Making P2P Legal

The EFF has proposed several ways to make P2P legal and pay the copyright owners. They have proposed advertising revenue sharing with the download sites, subscription costs to P2P service, and bandwidth levies (an extra charge to your Internet service provider). The money collected from any of these proposed sources would then be shared with artists, and Internet users would be protected from lawsuits.

This Boston library will have to install filtering technologies on its computers or risk losing funding.

FILTERING TECHNOLOGIES

The industries have put forth another solution to P2P networks. They have asked the networks to implement filtering software. This software would

block copyright material from
being shared on their networks.
RIAA representative Mitch Bainwol
points out that "many [peer to peer
networks] provide filters that at
least attempt to block pornography
and viruses."[4] Implementing filters
on the content should be a simple
addition to what P2P networks
already have in place.

"If P2P United's members wanted to become legitimate music download services, they could tomorrow. They've been running businesses for the last four years that have done nothing to get artists recompensed."[5]

– David Stuphin, RIAA vice president

Industry representatives are
looking to P2P networks to put these
roadblocks in place. They do not
feel that P2P vendors are doing enough to stop the
sharing of copyrighted material. Filters would be a step
toward ensuring that their networks are not being used
to share this material.

P2P vendors are reluctant to add these filters.
They do not feel it is their responsibility to manage
the content being shared on their networks. In
addition, they doubt that the proposed filters would
work on certain types of P2P networks. In their view,
filters would be a temporary and ineffective solution.
They predict that users would easily find a way around
the filters by encrypting the files. Filters would be

Bobby Kanaeaupuni encodes a film with copy protection for CinemaNow.

unable to identify these encrypted (concealed) files as copyrighted, and would not be able to stop them.

IMPROVE EXISTING SITES

There are already a number of legal Web sites available for Internet users to download content. However, many continue to use P2P networks because legal sites do not meet their standards. While iTunes boasts 3.5 million songs, there are still artists missing from their database. Internet users continue to search for this content elsewhere.

Legal downloading sites also receive complaints about poor quality recordings and the inability to use the files on other media. Some sites restrict the ways that their files can be used. Users may only be able to listen to music at their computers, or they may not be able to transfer music to other media devices.

"iTunes and other similar online stores provide a digital copy that is encoded at a quality far below that of CD and restricted in the rights that I have to use it."[6]

– Stephen Roberts, Birmingham, UK (Internet user)

Users are also dissatisfied with the prices. Consumers have begun to see the cost of CDs come down in stores. However, the cost to download an album online is sometimes higher than the cost of the actual album in stores. This is counterintuitive when consumers consider that they are physically getting less and would have to burn their own CDs.

During a six-week sale, online music downloading site Rhapsody dropped its price from 99 cents per song to 49 cents. During this time, the site sold three times as many downloads as it typically would have. If the industries were willing to adjust prices, consumers

might be more willing to pay for their music. Then
the industries could end up making even more of
a profit.

UNCERTAIN FUTURE

The issue of online file sharing may not be resolved
anytime soon. The industries continue to file lawsuits
against individual file sharers and P2P software
vendors. In addition, consumers continue to download
copyrighted material on peer-to-peer networks in
alarming numbers.

Until industries and consumers are able to make
some sort of compromise, P2P will continue to
flourish. Copyrighted files will continue to be shared
illegally. In the meantime, many of the decisions
about the future of P2P and copyright will be made
in the courts.

*Gabriel Lewenstein, left, and his brother, Ari, can put
up to 1,500 songs on their iPods.*

TIMELINE

1790	1886	1976
Congress enacts the first copyright law May 31, setting term limits at 14 years with a possibility of renewal for another 14 years.	Ten member countries of the Berne Convention in Switzerland sign "The Convention for the Protection of Literary and Artistic Works" September 9.	On October 19, Congress enacts the Copyright Act of 1976, setting copyright term limits at life plus 50 years, and introducing the Fair Use and First Sale Doctrines.

1988	1994	1996
The United States signs the Berne Convention November 16.	The Conference on Fair Use meets for the first time September 21 to discuss issues of fair use in the digital environment.	World Intellectual Property Organization members meet December 2 in Geneva, Switzerland, to discuss fair use in the digital environment.

1978	**1979**	**1984**
On July 31, the National Commission on New Technological Uses of Copyrighted Works (CONTU) creates guidelines for the "standards of educational fair use."	*Betamax* case goes to trial January 30.	*Betamax* case decided in favor of Sony January 17.

1997	**1998**	**1998**
President Clinton signs the No Electronic Theft Act (NET) into law December 16.	President Clinton signs the Sonny Bono Copyright Term Extension Act into law October 27.	President Clinton signs the Digital Millennium Copyright Act (DMCA) into law October 28.

TIMELINE

1999	1999	2003
The RIAA sues Napster for secondary copyright infringement December 8. The 9th Circuit Court of Appeals rules in favor of the RIAA and Napster is shut down.	The Senate approves the Digital Theft Deterrence and Copyright Damages Improvement Act July 1, raising the fine for copyright infringement.	The RIAA announces that it will begin gathering evidence against individual file sharers using P2P networks June 25.

2004	2005	2005
The MPAA announces its first wave of lawsuits against individual P2P filesharers November 16.	President Bush signs the Family Entertainment and Copyright Act into law April 27.	The United States Supreme Court rules against Grokster June 23 in *MGM Studios v. Grokster*.

2003

The RIAA announces the first wave of lawsuits against at least 261 individual file sharers on September 8.

2003

Brianna Lahara, a 12-year-old girl from New York, settles with the RIAA for $2,000 September 9.

2004

The RIAA announces 532 new "John Doe" lawsuits January 21.

2006

China's National Administration of Copyright (NAC) begins a three-month campaign September 30 to crack down on piracy of films, music, software, and textbooks.

2007

U.S. Representatives Rick Boucher and John Doolittle introduce the FAIR USE Act to Congress, February 27.

ESSENTIAL FACTS

AT ISSUE

Opposed

❖ Piracy is stealing.

❖ Internet users do not respect copyrights.

❖ File sharing results in profit losses for industries and artists.

❖ Profits lost will result in fewer jobs worldwide.

❖ Industries are not able to afford to produce albums by small artists.

❖ Consumers receive poor quality products through illegal downloading.

In Favor

❖ Reports of sales increases suggest piracy is not having a negative effect on industry profits.

❖ Independent software developers are limited in what they can achieve.

❖ Lesser-known artists can gain exposure online.

❖ The industries' reports are misleading.

❖ File sharing makes it easier to find rare files.

❖ Legal sites do not currently meet the needs of P2P users.

CRITICAL DATES

December 16, 1997
President Clinton signs the No Electronic Theft Act.

December 8, 1999
The RIAA sues Napster for secondary copyright infringement.

September 8, 2003
The RIAA announces the first wave of lawsuits against at least 261 individual file-sharers.

June 23, 2005
The U.S. Supreme Court rules against Grokster in *MGM Studios v. Grokster*.

QUOTES

Opposed
"The law is clear and the message to those who are distributing substantial quantities of music online should be equally clear—this activity is illegal, you are not anonymous when you do it, and engaging in it can have real consequences."—*Cary Sherman*

In Favor
"If 'piracy' means using the creative property of others without their permission … then the history of the content industry is a history of piracy. … The film industry of Hollywood was built by fleeing pirates."
— *Lawrence Lessig*

ADDITIONAL RESOURCES

SELECT BIBLIOGRAPHY

Kusek, David. *The Future of Music: Manifesto for the Digital Music Revolution*. Boston, MA: Berklee Press, 2005.

Lessig, Lawrence. *Free Culture*. New York: Penguin Press, 2004.

Litman, Jessica. *Digital Copyright*. Amherst, NY: Prometheus Press, 2001.

Martin, Scott. "The Mythology of the Public Domain: Exploring the Myths Behind Attacks on the Duration of Copyright Protection." *Loyola of Los Angeles Law Review*. 36 (2002): 253–322.

FURTHER READING

Lawler, Jennifer. *Cyberdanger and Internet Safety: A Hot Issue*. Berkeley Heights, NJ: Enslow Publishers, 2000.

Lougran, Donna. *Using the Internet Safely*. Chicago: Raintree, 2002.

Sherman, Josepha. *Internet Safety*. New York: Franklin Watts, 2003.

Toor, James. *At Issue Series: Internet Piracy*. Chicago: Greenhaven Press, 2004.

Whelan, Elaine and Copyrights Promote Creativity Project. "My Mom's Making History: The Story of Computer Software" *Copyrights and Creativity*, 2003.

Web Links

To learn more about Internet Piracy, visit ABDO Publishing Company on the World Wide Web at **www.abdopublishing.com**. Web sites about Internet Piracy are featured on our Book Links page. These links are routinely monitored and updated to provide the most current information available.

Places to Visit

Library of Congress
101 Independence Ave, SE, Washington, D.C. 20540
202-707-8000
www.loc.gov
The Library of Congress is home to the U.S. Copyright Office. Visitors can browse the library's collections and see the historic architecture.

U.S. Congress
Capitol Hill, Washington, D.C. 20540
202-225-6827
www.house.gov
The Capitol's Guide Service offers free guided tours to visitors.

The U.S. Supreme Court
Washington, D.C. 20543
202-479-3211
Many of the most important court decisions are made at the Supreme Court. Visitors can tour the building and participate in a variety of educational activities.

GLOSSARY

BitTorrent
> A type of P2P network designed to handle large files.

circumvention
> Finding a way around a problem.

Congress
> The legislative branch of U.S. government in charge of creating law, including copyright law.

copyright
> A set of rights given to the creator of a work such as a book, photograph, map, song, movie, video game, or software.

copyright infringement
> Violation of the exclusive rights of a copyright owner.

Darknet
> Servers, software, or networks used to distribute pirated works.

download
> To copy data from one computer to another.

exclusive right
> Sole ownership of something.

fair use
> The right to use copyrighted works without the copyright owner's permission for the purposes of criticism, comment, news reporting, teaching, scholarship, or research.

file sharing
> The transferring of computer files from one computer to another.

industry
> The people or companies that work in a particular kind of commercial business.

infringement
> Failure to obey a law or regulation.

intellectual property
> Creative works or ideas that can be owned through copyright.

Internet piracy
> Use of the Internet to violate the exclusive rights of copyright owners.

Internet service provider (ISP)
> A company that provides users with access to the Internet.

legislation
> Laws created by a legislative body.

license
> To give official permission to someone to do something that goes beyond the normal limits.

network
> A system of two or more computers, terminals, and communication devices connected to one another in order to share information.

open source
> Software that is licensed to allow the modification and redistribution of its source code.

peer-to-peer (P2P) network
> A computer network that connect users directly to other computers without going through a server.

public domain
> Works whose copyright term has expired.

server
> Computer or computer program that manages access to a central source.

software
> A program that tells a computer how to work.

streaming
> Transmitting data continuously so that the receiver can view or listen to the first parts of the file before the entire file is received.

Supreme Court
> The highest court in the United States.

upload
> To transfer data or programs from one computer to another.

Warez
> Pirated or illegally shared software.

SOURCE NOTES

Chapter 1. RIAA Lawsuits

1. "Recording Industry Begins Suing P2P File Sharers Who Illegally Offer Copyrighted Music Online." RIAA. 8 Sept. 2003. 28 Feb. 2007 <http://www.riaa.com/news/newsletter/090803.asp>.

2. "Issues: Anti-Piracy." RIAA. 28 Feb. 2007 <http://www.riaa.com/issues/piracy/default.asp>.

3. Ibid.

4. "Recording Industry To Begin Collecting Evidence And Preparing Lawsuits Against File 'Sharers' Who Illegally Offer Music Online." RIAA. 25 June 2003. 28 Feb. 2007 <http://www.riaa.com/news/newsletter/062503.asp>.

5. "Recording Industry Begins Suing P2P File Sharers Who Illegally Offer Copyrighted Music Online." RIAA. 8 Sept. 2003. 28 Feb. 2007 <http://www.riaa.com/news/newsletter/090803.asp>.

6. "Suits Could Backfire On Music Biz Industry's Legal Assault Could Drive Backlash Against It." *CBS News*. 10 Sept. 2003. 28 Feb. 2007 <http://www.cbsnews.com/stories/2003/09/16/tech/main573521.shtml>.

7. "Download Suit Targets 12-Year-Old: Girl's Mother Plans To Fight Music Industry's Lawsuit." *CBS News*. 9 Sep. 2003. 2 Feb. 2007 <http://www.nydailynews.com/front/story/116703p-105168c.html>.

8. Ibid.

Chapter 2. Understanding Copyright Law

1. United States. National Archives. United States Constitution. Washington: GPO. 20 Nov. 2006 <http://www.archives.gov/national-archives-experience/charters/

2. United States Copyright Office. Copyright Law- Chapter 1. Washington: GPO. 20. Nov. 2006 <http://www.copyright.gov/title17/92chap1.html>.

Chapter 3. Overview of the Controversy

1. United States. Congress House. Higher Education, Entertainment Industry Witnesses Detail Impact of, Efforts to Combat. 26 Sep. 2006. 22 Nov. 2006 <http://republicans.edlabor.house.gov/archive/press/press109/second/09sep/piracy092606.htm>.

2. Ibid.

3. Amy Harmon. "Black Hawk Download; Moving Beyond Music, Pirates Use New Tools to Turn the Net Into an Illicit Video Club." *New York Times* Online. 17 Jan. 2002. 22 Nov 2006 <http://tech2.nytimes.com/mem/technology/techreview.html?_r=2&res=9A04E2D91138F934A25752C0A9649C8B63&oref=slogin&oref=slogin>.

4. "What the Artists and Songwriters Have to Say." Musicunited.org. 22 Nov. 2006 <http://www.musicunited.org/3_artists.html>.

5. "Singer Lily Rose Allen on how she's profited from airing her music on MySpace." *The Observer.* 19 Mar. 2006. 19 Mar. 2007 <http://observer.guardian.co.uk/omm/story/0,,1733371,00.html>.

6. Neil Strauss. "File-Sharing Leaves Musicians Caught in Middle." *The New York Times.* 14 Sept. 2003. 19 March 2007 <http://www.nytimes.com/2003/09/14/technology/14MU.S.I.html?ex=1378872000&en=2832300e467debbe&ei=5007&partner=U.S.ERLAND>.

7. Jane Black. "Lawrence Lessig: The 'Dinosaurs' are Taking Over." BusinessWeek Online. 13 May 2002. 19 Mar. 2007 <http://www.businessweek.com/magazine/content/02_19/b3782610.htm>.

Chapter 4. Key Players in the Controversy

1. "About Us." RIAA. 28 Feb. 2007 <http://www.riaa.com/about/default.asp>.

2. "Recording Industry Begins Suing P2P File Sharers Who Illegally Offer Copyrighted Music Online." RIAA. 8 Sept. 2003. 28 Feb. 2007 <http://www.riaa.com/news/newsletter/090803.asp>.

3. "Members Page." MPAA. 15 Nov. 2006 <http://www.mpaa.org/AboutUsMembers.asp>.

SOURCE NOTES CONTINUED

4. United States. Congress. House. Committee on Ways and Means."Statement of Dan Glickman, Motion Picture Association of America." 21 Apr. 2005. 4 Mar. 2007 <http://waysandmeans.house.gov/hearings.asp?formmode=view&id=28 34>.

5. "About BSA." BSA. 18 Dec. 2006 <http://www.bsa.org/usa/about>.

6. "President's Welcome." BSA. 4 Mar. 2007 <http://www.bsa.org/usa/about/Presidents-Welcome.cfm>.

7. Lawrence Lessig. *Free Culture*. New York: Penguin Press, 2004. 13 Dec. 2006 <http://free-culture.org/freecontent/>.

8. "About Us." FSF. 4 Mar. 2007 <http://www.fsf.org/about>.

9. "Why Software Should Not Have Owners." GNU. 4 Mar. 2007 <http://www.gnu.org/philosophy/why-free.html>.

10. "About Us." Creative Commons. 4 Mar. 2007 <http://creativecommons.org/about/history>.

Chapter 5. Copyright in the Digital Age

1. "Statement of Business Software Alliance President and CEO Robert Holleyman concerning the first indictment and arraignment under the DMCA." BSA. 30 Aug. 2001. 18 Dec. 2006 <http://www.eff.org/IP/DMCA/unintended_consequences.php>.

2. Ibid.

3. Ibid.

Chapter 6. Online Technologies in Use

1. Jefferson Graham. "Court cases don't scare music file swappers away." *USA Today*. 6 Sept. 2005. 5 Dec. 2005 <http://www.usatoday.com/tech/products/services/2005-09-06-file-swapping_x.htm>

2. "Music Industry Commences New Wave of Legal Action Against Illegal File Sharers." RIAA. 3 Dec. 2003. 8 Dec. 2006

<http://www.riaa.com/news/newsletter/120303.asp>.

3. "Universal hits MySpace with copyright suit." CNN.com. 17 Nov 2006. 30 Nov. 2006 <http://money.cnn.com/2006/11/17/technology/universal_myspace.reut/index.htm>.

Chapter 7. P2P in the Courts

1. "Legal Cases." RIAA. 5 Dec. 2006 <http://www.riaa.com/news/filings/default.asp>.

Chapter 8. Avoiding Piracy

1. "Los Angeles Area Boy Scouts Collaborate with MPAA to Teach Young People About Respecting Copyrights." MPAA. 20 Oct. 2006. 15 Nov. 2006   <http://www.mpaa.org/PressReleases.asp>.

2. "RIAA Issues 2005 Year-End Shipment Numbers." RIAA. 31 March 2006. 19 Dec. 2006 <http://www.riaa.com/news/newsletter/033106.asp>.

Chapter 9. Solutions That Bridge the Gap

1. "Online music lovers 'frustrated.'" *BBC News*. 25 Apr. 2005. 20 Dec. 2006. 19 Mar. 2007 <http://news.bbc.co.uk/1/hi/technology/4474143.stm>.

2. Grant Gross. "RIAA Opposes Fair Use bill" *PC World*. 28 Feb. 2007 <http://www.pcworld.com/article/id,129465/article.html>.

3. "A better way forward: Voluntary Collective Licensing of music file sharing." EFF. 2004. 19 Mar. 2007 <http://www.eff.org/share/collective_lic_wp.pdf >.

4. Mitch Bainwol. "Privacy & Piracy: The Paradox of Illegal file sharing on peer-to-peer networks and the impact of the technology on the entertainment industry" RIAA. 30 Sept. 2003. 19 Mar. 2007 <http://www.riaa.com/news/newsletter/093003_2a.asp >.

5. Grant Gross. "P2P Vendors Say Let the Music Play." *PC World*. 26 Feb. 2004. 19 Mar. 2007 <http://www.pcworld.com/article/id,114994-page,1/article.html>.

6. "Online music lovers 'frustrated'." *BBC News*. 25 Apr. 2005. 20 Dec. 2006 <http://news.bbc.co.uk/1/hi/technology/4474143.stm>.

INDEX

ABOUT THE AUTHOR

Lee Hunnewell is a former social studies teacher. She has worked in Colombia, Switzerland, Zambia, and Turkey, both as a teacher and curriculum designer. Her main pedagogic goal is to help students think through complex issues for themselves. No longer in the classroom, she pursues this objective as a freelance writer and editor for educational publishing houses.

PHOTO CREDITS

AP Images, cover, 64; Frank Rumpenhorst/AP Images, 3; Kathy Mclaughlin/AP Images, 6, 99 (top); Pablo Martinez Monsivais/AP Images, 9; Paul Sakuma, 17, 70, 81, 96; Tammie Arroyo, 18, 97 (bottom); Greg Gibson/AP Images, 27; Gerald Herbert/AP Images, 28, 73; The State Press, Ashley Lowery/AP Images, 39, 98; George Nikitin/AP Images, 40; Damian Dovarganes/AP Images, 42; Paul Chiasson, CP/AP Images, 51; Thomas Terry/AP Images, 52; Bullit Marquez/AP Images, 59, 99 (bottom); Greg Baker/AP Images, 60; Noah Berger/AP Images, 67; Peter Lennihan/AP Images, 68; Jae C. Hong/AP Images, 77; Sandy Huffaker/AP Images, 78; Kevin P. Casey/AP Images, 85; Ted S. Warren/AP Images, 86; Chitose Suzuki/AP Images, 90; Ric Francis/AP Images, 92; Marcio Jose Sanchez/AP Images, 95.